Mr. Lincoln and the Time Train

Written by WeWrite Kids

Erika Brodland
Sierra Brodland
Tyler Cameron
Emma Frederick
Kamaria Gage
Isiah Hale
Alyssa Henson
Lonnie Lucas
Glen Morrison
Joseph Stowell
Samuel Stowell
Linna Vo
Mily Vo
Matthew Wilde

for

ABRAHAM LINCOLN
PRESIDENTIAL CENTER FOR GOVERNMENTAL STUDIES

UNIVERSITY *of* ILLINOIS *at* SPRINGFIELD

ISBN: 0-938943-21-9

This story is the result of a workshop conducted by the WeWrite Corporation on behalf of the Abraham Lincoln Presidential Center for Governmental Studies held at the Lincoln Library in Springfield, Illinois on November 15 – 16, 2002. Richard F. (Fritz) Klein of the Lincoln Institute For Education, Inc. portrayed President Lincoln at the workshop on November 15, 2002.

Workshop book-writing process facilitated by WeWrite Corporation:
   1-800-295-9037 • www.wewrite.net
Cover and story illustrations (unless noted): Charles Goll, www.fallingsanta.com
Book design and layout: Rita Brodland, WeWrite Corporation
Photos:Robert Andrews, WeWrite staff and UIS staff
Editors: Rita Brodland, WeWrite Corporation; and Rodd Whelpley, UIS
Printer: MultiAd, Inc., Peoria, IL, www.multiad.com

Printed in the United States of America

10 9 8 7 6 5 4 3 2 1

Center Publications
Abraham Lincoln Presidential Center
   for Governmental Studies
University of Illinois at Springfield
Human Resources Building, 10
One University Plaza, HRB 10
Springfield, IL 62703-5407

Phone: 217-206-6502
Fax: 217-206-7257
e-mail: whelpley.rodd@uis.edu
Web site: http://alpcgs.uis.edu

UNIVERSITY *of* ILLINOIS *at* SPRINGFIELD

Special Acknowledgements

Thank you to everyone who supported the undertaking of this book about Abraham Lincoln written by kids, for kids!

Parents and chaperones of the co-authors, thank you for providing such bright and insightful kids, for bringing them to the workshop, for being scribes, and for supporting literacy for all.

Ernest L. Cowles, PhD, interim executive director of the Abraham Lincoln Presidential Center for Governmental Studies, and **Barbara E. Ferrara,** associate director of the Abraham Lincoln Presidential Center for Governmental Studies, for their vision and support for the project.

Daniel Stowell, director of the Papers of Abraham Lincoln, for fact checking the manuscript.

Kelly Phillips of the Abraham Lincoln Presidential Center for Governmental Studies for her exact transcription of the WeWrite workshop.

Robert W. Raleigh of the Abraham Lincoln Presidential Center for Governmental Studies for handling accounting and contractual details.

Larz Gaydos, UIS campus services print production coordinator, for technical advice and making arrangements with our printer.

Michael Morsch, publisher of Center Publications at the Abraham Lincoln Presidential Center for Governmental Studies, for supporting the project and freeing up staff time to devote to *Mr. Lincoln and the Time Train.*

Kathleen G. Walter and Principal Tracy Gage at Laketown Elementary School for helping arrange co-author participation.

Lincoln Library for providing the workshop venue in support of literacy.

Springfield Illinois Convention & Visitors Bureau for their support and flexibility in scheduling.

Meet Fido!

When Abraham Lincoln lived in Springfield, Illinois, his family had a dog, cats, a horse, chickens, and a cow. The cats kept mice away, the horse provided transportation, and the chickens laid eggs. The cow grazed on an empty lot behind the Lincoln home and provided fresh milk for the family.

But the Lincoln children loved to play with their dog, Fido, best of all. He was one of Mr. Lincoln's favorite pets!

In this story, Fido helps readers by explaining some of the story's details. Look for President Lincoln's curious dog throughout the book "digging deeper" to help everyone understand many of the terms and historical facts.

Mr. Lincoln and the Time Train

It would be a long day, and Abraham Lincoln knew it. He was on a train going to Pennsylvania to speak at the dedication of a battleground. Lots of soldiers from both sides had died fighting at Gettysburg, and a part of the field was going to be made into a national cemetery. Mr. Lincoln had been asked to speak at the dedication. He was thinking about his speech. It was tucked into his beaver hat sitting on the seat next to him.

Fido Digs Deeper

A beaver hat is a tall hat covered in silk or fur—some people call them "stove-pipe" hats because they're tall and straight, like the top of an old stove pipe.

The Civil War was terribly hard on the United States. Abraham Lincoln knew that if the Confederate States had their way, they would become their own country. It made Mr. Lincoln sad to think that some of the states that had joined together to form America would break their promise to be united. After all, united meant together – not apart. If the Confederates won the war, it would no longer be the United States.

He was also worried about the spread of slavery. Mr. Lincoln did not believe in keeping people as property – forcing them to work without pay. He thought back to his own "emancipation."

Fido Digs Deeper

Abraham Lincoln wrote the Emancipation Proclamation in 1862 and signed the orders on January 1, 1863. In 1865, the 13th Amendment to the Constitution ended slavery everywhere in the United States. Illinois was the first state to ratify, or approve, the law.

When he finally became old enough, the money he earned from his job no longer went to his father. He was free to work and live on his own. Emancipation means "freedom."

As president, Abraham Lincoln had already written the Emancipation Proclamation, declaring that all slaves in the Confederate States were free.

But many states ignored that idea. Maybe, when the Union won the war…

The old locomotive rattled down the tracks, blowing smoke and rocking. Clickity-clack, clickity-clack, clickity-clack, chug, chug, chug… the president thought he'd close his eyes, just for a moment. The wood stove in the back of the President's special train car made it toasty warm on the chilly November day. Abraham Lincoln fell asleep.

Mr. Lincoln's chin hit his chest, and he shook himself as he woke up. He wasn't on a train anymore; he was sitting on a bench outside of a big building. It was sunny, but the wind was cold. He shook his head and tried to figure out where he was. He picked up his hat, put it on his head, and stood up.

"Where am I?" he thought. "This place looks strange."

Three kids were walking toward him. A little girl with dark, braided hair whispered. "That looks like Abraham Lincoln!"

"Who do you think I should look like?" the president asked.

The girl's brown eyes grew bigger when the man spoke.

"Don't worry, he can't be real," said a tall, blue-eyed boy in a long black coat. "That can't be Abraham Lincoln."

"You know my name? How do you know my name?" asked the president.

"Because you're famous," exclaimed another little girl in a fuzzy red jacket. "Look up!"

Mr. Lincoln took off his hat and leaned back as he read the words on the building in front of him. "Abraham Lincoln Presidential Library. A library with my name on it? Oh my! Why would such an important-looking place have my name on it?" Mr. Lincoln said. He put his hat back on with a smile. He seemed pleased.

Angela, the girl with the braids, hid behind her tall friend with blue eyes — a boy named Ryan. Angela, Ryan and Jennifer, the girl with the fuzzy red jacket, were on their way to the library to do a report. The three friends looked at each other, wondering what to do next. Could this really be Abraham Lincoln?

They stared at the tall man dressed in black. He was wearing a beard with no moustache. He sure looked like Mr. Lincoln. He wore clothes like Mr. Lincoln used to wear. He even had the stove-pipe hat! But he was looking around now, tugging at his beard as if he were worried.

"Where's the battlefield? Where are all the soldiers?" the president asked. "Isn't this Gettysburg? I'm supposed to give a speech today."

"No, Mr. Lincoln – you're in Springfield, Illinois," said Jennifer. "Gettysburg is in Pennsylvania. That's pretty far from here. You're supposed to deliver a speech today?"

Ryan studied the man carefully. "The Civil War is already over," he blurted out.

"The Civil War is over? How is the war over? Who won?"

The children all looked at each other, smiling. "We did!"

"We? The Confederacy or the Union?" the president asked, still puzzled. "The South or the North?"

Ryan decided this man must be Abraham Lincoln. He whispered to the others, "I think it really is him." Then he answered Mr. Lincoln proudly, because he knew the answer. "Oh, the North won."

Fido Digs Deeper

A "civil war" is when people from one country fight against each other. The Northern States were known as the Union, and they fought to keep the country together. The Southern States were known as the Confederacy. They fought for their right to secede, or drop out, of the United States and become their own country.

"Yippee!" cried Mr. Lincoln as he jumped up in the air. The kids laughed that a grown-up would do that. "That means there are still 35 states," he said.

"Well, actually, there are now 50 states. Count the stars on the flag!" Angela pointed to the American flag flying above them.

Abraham Lincoln knew that a star was being added to the flag every time a new state was admitted to the Union. "Fifty states?" he questioned. It was hard to believe. The president had been worried that even when the Civil War ended the North and South would not get along. "So, we're still the United States?"

"Sure we are! Thanks to you," Ryan said with a grin.

"Me? I'm nothing special. Surely not special enough for all this fuss," Lincoln said in disbelief as he pointed at the big building.

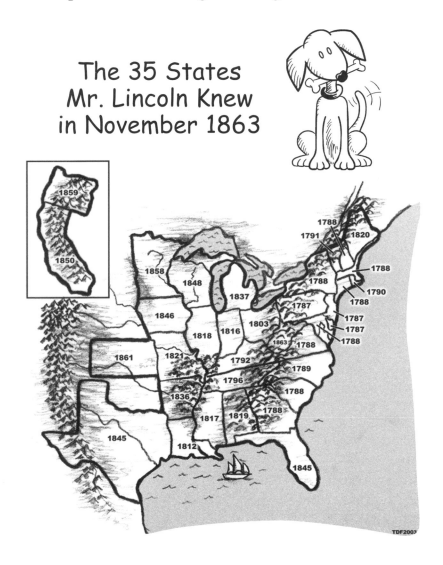

The 35 States
Mr. Lincoln Knew
in November 1863

Angela moved closer to Mr. Lincoln and looked very seriously at the tall man. "You stopped slavery," she said quietly. "If it weren't for you, I…" her words trailed off. There were tears in her eyes. The president leaned down and put his arms around the girl to comfort her.

Abraham Lincoln did not like the idea of slavery. He knew that some people owned slaves and treated them like property. They were forced to work for no pay. When he was a young boy, he had seen blood on the road near his family's farm.

It had come from a group of slaves who had been forced to walk down that road with metal shackles  clamped around their ankles. The metal cut into their skin and made the slaves bleed. Even though it hurt, they couldn't do anything about it. They had to keep moving, chained to each other.

Another time he saw slaves being sold. He saw a young couple who looked like they were in love, waiting for a boat in St. Louis. The man who owned them decided that he needed some extra money. So just before the boat came, the man sold the young wife to someone else. Her new husband got very upset. The woman cried and begged, "No! No! No! We just got ourselves married! Don't do that to us!" But the man sold her anyway. Seeing that had made Mr. Lincoln feel just awful. It wasn't fair.

But now, here was this little dark-skinned girl, out walking with her two friends. Maybe slavery didn't exist anymore! The president didn't know what to say, so he hugged the girl some more.

Afraid everyone would start to cry, Ryan figured he'd better make everyone laugh instead. "Man, you're as tall as two of me and three of her!"

Fido Digs Deeper

Abraham Lincoln once described himself as "six feet four inches tall, once I get the kinks out." He is the tallest president in United States history.

"Yeah, right!" said Jennifer. Everyone laughed.

The president looked around again. So many strange looking things — and the way people dressed! Well, he knew that it wasn't 1863 any more. He asked the kids, "What year is it?"

Angela answered, "It's 2003."

Mr. Lincoln froze for a second in shock then he smacked his head with his hand. "I can't believe it!"

"But it's true, Mr. Lincoln," Ryan explained. "And this Library here is a special place full of things you've written or said, and it has tons of books about you."

Angela grabbed his hand. "You've got to come see it!"

All three kids pulled the president into the Abraham Lincoln Presidential Library, and his mouth fell open when he saw all the books. "Books about me?

Well, I'll be." Mr. Lincoln asked. "Are you sure?"

"Sure we're sure. Come see!" Jennifer pulled the president toward a shelf full of books. All three kids gathered around as the president took down a book and flipped through the pages.

"I remember that!" he cried, pointing at a picture.

"And this is a picture of you during the Civil War," said Angela, pointing toward another drawing. "You seem sad there."

"I *was* sad," said Mr. Lincoln. "It's a sad time for our whole country. I know that some of the border states — the states on the edges of the North and the South — some of those states have a hard time deciding what to do. Cousins end up fighting against their own cousins, and brothers against their brothers. It's awful." Mr. Lincoln paused and sat down. He took off his beaver hat and placed it on his knee. His arms rested on the sides of the chair, but Abraham Lincoln sat tall, staring straight ahead.

Angela could see that the Civil War was really hard on the president. He seemed so tired and sad. She wanted to make him feel better, but she didn't know what to say.

Ryan broke the quiet. "I fight with my brothers all the time. But I still love them." He couldn't imagine how it would feel to actually kill his own brother — or anyone. It was hard to think about.

Angela put her small hand over Mr. Lincoln's big hand and quietly said, "You did and said the right things, Mr. President. After all, remember what you said? 'A house divided against itself cannot stand.' Would either country — the Union or Confederacy — be half as strong as the entire United States of America?"

A smile began to spread across the president's face and he put his other hand over Angela's. "I do remember saying that. I didn't believe that our country would last being half slave and half free. I suppose you've heard about that speech, have you, Angela?"

Abraham Lincoln gave a famous speech on June 16, 1858 when he was chosen by the state Republican convention to run for the U.S. Senate. This is the main idea of Mr. Lincoln's "House Divided" Speech:

"A house divided against itself cannot stand."

I believe this government cannot endure, permanently half *slave* and half *free*.

I do not expect the Union to be *dissolved* — I do not expect the house to *fall* — but I *do* expect it will cease to be divided.

It will become *all* one thing, or *all* the other.

Either the *opponents* of slavery, will arrest the further spread of it, and place it where the public mind shall rest in the belief that it is in the course of ultimate extinction; or its *advocates* will push it forward, till it shall become alike lawful in *all* the States, *old* as well as *new* — *North* as well as *South*.

Angela smiled warmly. Yes, she knew that speech. When she read it, she had pictured a house falling apart. But when he gave that speech, President Lincoln was facing his country falling apart. He believed that it would become either all slave, or all free. And he wanted it to be all free. What might have happened if someone else had become president? Angela squeezed Mr. Lincoln's hand, and he smiled warmly at her.

Jennifer brought another book to the president, and he looked through the pages with great interest.

"Everything is so easy to see. What sort of fancy candles are these? The light is so steady and bright!" Mr. Lincoln pointed to the lights above him, just then realizing that it was more than daylight and candlelight making the room bright.

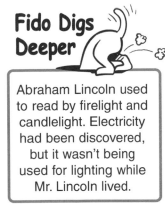

Fido Digs Deeper

Abraham Lincoln used to read by firelight and candlelight. Electricity had been discovered, but it wasn't being used for lighting while Mr. Lincoln lived.

Ryan broke into a big smile. "A man named Thomas Edison figured out a way to make light using electricity. It's really changed how this country does things!" he said proudly.

Ryan was interested in stuff like that. He even hoped that one day he might be an inventor! He happened to know that Abraham Lincoln is the only president to hold a patent. Lincoln had invented a device to get boats free from sandbars, but it was never produced. Still, Ryan thought that it was pretty cool that Mr. Lincoln was an inventor, too.

The next picture was a drawing of Abraham Lincoln standing on a platform giving a speech. The caption under the picture said Gettysburg Address. The president's eyes lit up. "Last thing I remember, I was on my way to Gettysburg. I'm supposed to give a speech there."

Fido Digs Deeper

Cameras were around during the Civil War, but there were far more drawings and paintings of the war than actual photographs.

Jennifer began to worry. "If you're here, how will you give that speech? The Gettysburg Address really meant a lot to people. You never know what might happen if you don't say that speech."

But Mr. Lincoln was still looking at the picture. "So I gave the speech, did I? It wasn't much. Did people like it?"

Ryan shrugged his shoulders and answered honestly, "Some liked it, and some didn't."

Lincoln laughed, "That figures." He reached in his hat and found an early version of the speech. "Here it is!" he said, happy that it was still there. He put his hat back on with the speech inside.

"Let's read some more. This is fun!" Angela said as she ran back to the shelf for more books.

Mr. Lincoln and the children sat in the library reading and looking at books. The president told the kids stories about the pictures they saw.

In another book, the kids found the same picture they'd seen earlier of Abraham Lincoln at Gettysburg. But something was different now.

"Look," said Ryan. "There's some sort of hole in the book. And the picture is moving now. That's weird!"

"You're right," said Jennifer. "But look! Someone else is talking."

"That's Edward Everett," said President Lincoln, shaking his head. "That man can talk for hours."

Angela pointed to another man in the picture. He was walking back and forth near the platform. "But that person looks worried. Do you know who that is?" she asked.

Fido Digs Deeper

Edward Everett, one of the most famous speakers of the time, spoke for two hours at Gettysburg before Lincoln gave his speech. The crowd was standing the whole time!

The next day, Everett sent a note to Mr. Lincoln that said,

"I should be glad, if I could flatter myself that I came as near to the central idea of the occasion, in two hours, as you did in two minutes."

"That's the governor of Pennsylvania, Andrew Curtain," said Mr. Lincoln. "I expect he's wondering where I am."

Ryan pushed another book in front of the president. "Look at this!" he said.

The president scrunched up his eyes and put his face very close to the picture. "It seems to be a newspaper headline," he said.

"It says 'Lincoln Missing,'" read Jennifer. "It's from November 1863."

Ryan looked around at the shelves. His mouth fell open and his eyes got big. "Weren't there more books here earlier?"

Angela's feet suddenly felt cold. She looked down and saw that her shoes were missing. The nice, neat clothes she had put on that morning were gone. Now her clothes were torn and dirty.

"Look at Angela!" said Jennifer. "What's happening to her?"

Angela stared at the open book on the table in front of her. The letters didn't make sense to her any more. "I can't read!" she said. "What's going on?" She was scared. She put her face in her hands and began to cry. Jennifer went to comfort her friend.

A tall, angry looking man stomped over to Angela. "You have to leave, little girl," he said. He gave Jennifer a very mean look, but Jennifer stuck her chin out and kept her arm around Angela.

Angela cried even harder, but Mr. Lincoln stood up to the man. "She can stay. This is my library," he said loudly.

"But I run this library. She's colored and she has to get out."

"That's not nice! And besides, it doesn't matter what color her skin is," Ryan protested.

The man ignored Ryan and pointed at the door. "Get out! Get out! You can't be in here. No coloreds allowed!"

Lincoln put his hat on his head angrily. "Come on, children. I won't stay in a library where all people aren't treated as equals."

As the group walked out the door, Jennifer noticed that more and more books were disappearing. She was scared now, too. Her arm was still around Angela's shoulder. "It's like history is changing," she whispered.

Fido Digs Deeper

It took a long time for some to accept that people with "colored skin" should have the same rights as everyone else. Even after slaves were set free, many were not treated fairly. People like Martin Luther King, Jr. had to fight for "civil rights" long after the Civil War.

The children stood outside in front of the library. It wasn't as beautiful as it was before. There weren't as many people, and things just seemed sort of gray. Angela tried to stop crying.

"I think Jennifer's right," said Ryan. "I think history is changing." He noticed that there weren't as many buildings, or nearly as many cars. Things were definitely different.

"Is that why I'm dressed like this? Why I can't read?" It was hard for Angela to say the words. She was trying to wipe her tears.

Abraham Lincoln got very quiet for a moment. He crossed his arms in front of his chest, then reached up and slowly scratched his beard.

"I think it's because you got lost," said Ryan. "You were supposed to give a speech at Gettysburg and you never made it. Remember the newspaper headline we saw when everything got all weird?"

Fido Digs Deeper

Very few plantation owners were interested in eduction beyond teaching slaves what they needed to know to do their jobs. However, many slaves secretly learned how to read and write, and they taught their children in hopes of a better life.

"I think you're right, son," the Mr. Lincoln said. "If I'm here, I guess that means I'm not there. I worked hard to become President of the United States." He seemed sad and tired.

"Maybe there aren't any United States. Maybe the Union didn't win the war," said Jennifer.

"And maybe, slavery…" stuttered Angela. But she was too afraid to finish her sentence.

"This is what life might be like without you," Jennifer said to Lincoln. She frowned.

"We've got to get you back!" cried Ryan.

What do you think the map would look like if the Southern states had been allowed to secede?

UNITED STATES OF AMERICA

CONFEDERATE STATES OF AMERICA

TDF 2003

Lincoln agreed with the kids. As much as he loved seeing how his old hometown of Springfield had changed, he knew that he didn't belong in 2003. He and the kids knew he had to get back to 1863. They tried to figure out what to do to send the president back.

"What's the last thing you remember before you got here?" asked Angela.

"I was on the train on the way to Gettysburg. I remember it was warm. I sat there for a spell, but I must have dozed off. When I woke up, I was here."

"You were near that bench when we saw you," said Jennifer.

"That's where I woke up," said Lincoln.

"Maybe that's the key," said Ryan. "Maybe if you would just sit down on that bench and fall back asleep…"

Angela finished his sentence. "You'd wake up back on the train!"

"Here, Mr. Lincoln. Sit down," said Jennifer as she tugged on the president's sleeve.

Abraham Lincoln sat on the bench.

He stared at the children.

They stared at him.

"Well?" asked Mr. Lincoln.

"Go to sleep," suggested Ryan.

Mr. Lincoln closed his eyes and waited. After a while he opened one eye and peeked at the kids. "Am I asleep yet?" he asked.

"No," said Angela. "You're still here."

"I want to fall asleep and go home. I just can't seem to get sleepy," said Lincoln. He took a deep breath then puffed his cheeks and let it out slowly. He was frustrated and worried, but not sleepy.

"But you've got to go back," said Angela. "You've got to fix history." She wiggled her cold toes.

Jennifer bent down and put her gloves on Angela's feet. She was in the mood to solve problems. "We've got to help the president get to sleep," decided Jennifer.

"But how?" asked Mr. Lincoln.

"Well, I get sleepy after I eat a big meal. Maybe he should eat something," Ryan suggested.

Angela stood on one foot. She shivered from the cold. "Ryan, I don't think we have time for that. Besides, where are we going to get food? Do you think anyone will let me in like this?" She switched and stood on the other foot, rubbing her arms trying to keep warm. She could see a sign on a nearby business that said NO COLOREDS.

Jennifer saw the sign, too. "We've got to think! What makes someone fall asleep?" She tapped the side of her head with her finger. "When I had my tonsils out they used a gas to put me to sleep," she said. "But we can't very well take Abraham Lincoln to the hospital, can we?"

The president squinted his eyes. He thought about the many homes and barns that were turned into hospitals to take care of soldiers injured on battlegrounds.

Suddenly President Lincoln was in a big hurry. "I have to go back, right now! Ryan, maybe you could knock me out."

Ryan's eyes got big. He looked at the great man in front of him. "Well, maybe I could bump you on the head with a book or something," he offered.

The president shook his head to agree, but Jennifer put a stop to that, stepping between them. "Ryan, you can't do that. This is the 16th president of the United States!" said Jennifer. She rolled her eyes.

"Yes, be respectful," said Angela.

Abraham Lincoln smiled at his new friend. He knew in his heart that if he went back, then she would be able to read again and have nice clothes and be treated with respect, no matter what color her skin was. Something that he said or did in the past had made a difference. Slavery would end.

Fido Digs Deeper

During the Civil War, it was too difficult to carry injured soldiers a long distance to treat them. Battles were fought in fields, and nearby houses and barns would be used as hospitals and for shelter. Since most able-bodied men were out fighting, often the only people left in those homes were women and children. They would end up taking care of the hurt and dying men whether they wanted to or not.

Ryan thought that if he had some time he could probably invent a time machine. But time was something they didn't have. He knew that President Lincoln somehow had to relax and fall asleep, just as he had on the train.

"Let's sing him a lullaby," suggested Jennifer.

"Nahh," said Ryan. "I have a better idea. Let's get him a pillow and some blankets to keep him warm."

"Yeah, right!" said Jennifer. "Where are we going to find pillows and blankets in the middle of downtown Springfield?"

"Use your coats," suggested Angela. She didn't have one, but the other kids did.

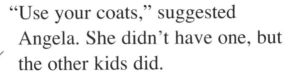

Ryan shook off his long, black coat and put it on the president. Jennifer took her fuzzy red jacket and tucked it under Mr. Lincoln's chin and around his shoulders.

"How's that?" asked Ryan.

"I'm getting warmer," said Mr. Lincoln with a little smile.

"What else could we do to help you sleep?" asked Jennifer.

"Maybe a story or something," the president said, trying to be helpful. "Do you know one?"

The children huddled together to keep warm while they thought.

"I know," said Angela. "Maybe if we said the Gettysburg Address…"

"You mean my speech for the dedication?" asked Mr. Lincoln. "Do you know it? That would make me feel good."

All of the children had already memorized the speech for class. "Of course we know it!" they assured him.

Fido Digs Deeper

Abraham Lincoln probably had to learn how to sleep whether he was comfortable or not. In his time, mattresses would sometimes be stuffed with scratchy straw or feathers. Plus, beds were shorter than they are today, and Mr. Lincoln was very tall. And, when he rode the circuit as a lawyer, he often had to share a bed with another lawyer.

"Four score and seven years ago, our fathers brought forth upon this continent," Jennifer began.

Angela and Ryan closed their eyes and joined in. Abraham Lincoln closed his eyes, too.

The version of the Gettysburg Address on the following pages is the same as the handwritten copy that is held by the Illinois State Historical Library.

⟶

When the children were finished saying the speech, they looked to where Abraham Lincoln sat. But there was nothing on the bench but their coats.

The Gettysburg Address

Four score and seven years ago our fathers brought forth upon this continent, a new nation, conceived in liberty, and dedicated to the proposition that all men are created equal.

Now we are engaged in a great civil war, testing whether that nation, or any nation so conceived, and so dedicated, can long endure. We are met on a great battle-field of that war. We have come to dedicate a portion of that field, as a final resting place for those who here gave their lives, that that nation might live. It is altogether fitting and proper that we should do this.

But, in a larger sense, we cannot dedicate — we cannot consecrate — we cannot hallow — this ground. The brave men, living and dead, who struggled here, have consecrated it, far above our poor power to add or detract. The world will little note, nor long remember, what we say here, but it can never forget what they did here. It is for us, the living, rather, to be dedicated here to the unfinished work which they who fought here, have, thus far, so nobly advanced. It is rather for us to be here dedicated to the great task remaining before us — that from these honored dead we take increased devotion to that cause for which they here gave the last full measure of devotion — that we here highly resolve that these dead shall not have died in vain — that this nation, under God, shall have a new birth of freedom — and that, government of the people, by the people, for the people, shall not perish from the earth.

"He's gone," said Ryan. "Maybe it worked!"

"Angela, look — your clothes are back to normal! Can you read again?" asked Jennifer.

"Let's go inside and find out," said Angela. "Let's see if the history books are back to normal too."

The three kids hurried inside the Abraham Lincoln Presidential Library.

The tall man greeted them at the door. He seemed friendly now. "Welcome," he said, "How may I help you?"

"We have to do a report on Abraham Lincoln," said Ryan. "Do you have books on him?"

"Do we?" the tall man said with a laugh. "Just look around!"

Angela bravely stepped forward. "Do you have a book that I can look at?"

"I'm sure we do," he answered. "Is there anything in particular you want to know?"

Angela just smiled. She knew everything she needed to already, she thought. Words made sense again. And she knew that no matter what color her skin was, she was welcome at the Abraham Lincoln Presidential Library.

The children looked around. The shelves were filled. Surely there were enough books for a thousand reports on Abraham Lincoln, but Ryan, Jennifer, and Angela knew they wouldn't need them. They had talked to Abraham Lincoln and knew what life could be like if he hadn't been president.

Without saying anything more, they looked at each other, then sat down to begin writing their amazing story. "President Lincoln was on a train heading to Gettysburg...."

ABOUT THE ABRAHAM LINCOLN PRESIDENTIAL CENTER FOR GOVERNMENTAL STUDIES

The Abraham Lincoln Presidential Center for Governmental Studies is a public policy center of the University of Illinois at Springfield. Affiliated with the Abraham Lincoln Presidential Library and Museum, the Center:

- Researches, evaluates, and helps form effective public policy,

- Educates citizens on public affairs issues,

- Promotes literacy in America, and

- Provides leadership and professional development programs.

The Center carries forward the legacy of Abraham Lincoln by applying the lessons of his leadership and his era to contemporary issues. As the academic arm of the Abraham Lincoln Presidential Library and Museum, the Center provides a national stage for scholars, students, policymakers, and citizens to exchange ideas, engage in research, and expand our understanding of public policy issues.

The Center is composed of the **Office of the Executive Director** along with nine other Center units, which are:

- *Illinois Issues* **magazine and Center Publications:** Publishing the state's leading public affairs magazine and books on Illinois politics and public policy.

- **The Institute for Leadership, Policy Education, and Training:** Preparing public policymakers for the future and informing citizens about how government works.

- **The Institute for Legal, Administrative, and Policy Studies:** Helping government entities develop and implement effective policies and programs; and focusing research and service efforts on state, regional, and national legal systems.

- **The Institute for Legislative Studies:** Generating and disseminating information on the legislative process and state politics to policymakers, political scientists, and the public.

- **The Institute for Literacy in America:** Providing the leadership to establish Illinois as a model for literacy in America.

- **The Office of Electronic Media:** Using video, audio, and emerging communication technologies to support the Center's teaching and public affairs mission.

- **The Papers of Abraham Lincoln:** Working to provide anyone with Internet access the ability to view, search, and analyze all the papers of America's greatest president.

- **The Survey Research Office:** Offering a full range of survey research services and selected data management services to government agencies and nonprofit organizations.

- **WUIS/WIPA:** Broadcasting public radio to central and western Illinois at 91.9 and 89.3 FM.

In addition to these units, the Center operates:

- The Graduate Public Service Internship Program

- The Illinois Legislative Staff Internship Program

- Other internship, fellowship, and grant programs

On the web at http://alpcgs.uis.edu

Fritz Klein as Mr. Lincoln

The Abraham Lincoln Presidential Center for Governmental Studies at the University of Illinois at Springfield commissioned a special guest to help the co-authors get started.

Richard F. (Fritz) Klein is considered by many to be one of the nation's foremost Lincoln actors. He has appeared in 35 states and been invited to perform in five countries. Mr. Klein has portrayed Abraham Lincoln at conventions, trade shows, civil war reenactments, and on film, television, and stage. He also performs as a motivational speaker.

A professional actor since 1980, and having the same height, weight, and physical appearance of Abraham Lincoln himself, he brings both professionalism and realism to the role. Using Mr. Lincoln's own style of public speaking, his performances move and breathe with a sense that one is seeing and hearing the real thing. The audience experiences the uncanny resemblance as well as the speech patterns, mannerisms, and original words. Fritz Klein captivates with the familiar eloquence, wit, and homespun humor of Abraham Lincoln.

For more information about **Lincoln Actor Richard F. Klein,** call **1-800-746-4223,** visit **www.lincolninstitute.com,** or write **Klein@LincolnInstitute.com.**

Abraham Lincoln Returns to Springfield!

(Well, sort of.)

On November 16, 2002, fourteen children gathered at a special book-writing workshop at Lincoln Library in Springfield, Illinois. The workshop was sponsored by the Abraham Lincoln Presidential Center for Governmental Studies at the University of Illinois at Springfield. Below is a kid's perspective of what went on and how the book you are holding came to be.

We were a bunch of kids ranging in age from 7 to 10 years old. All we knew was that we'd been invited to become authors, writing a book about Abraham Lincoln. When we first arrived at Lincoln Library, we each got nametags so we could get to know each other. WeWrite Corporation was running the workshop, and they had chairs all set up and a microphone. We were all a little nervous, but excited, too.

We were very impressed when Abraham Lincoln walked in and introduced himself! Actually, we had been told that well-known interpreter Fritz Klein would be talking to us as if he were Mr. Lincoln. It was easy to believe, because Mr. Klein looks and acts so much like our 16th president. He told stories and answered questions, helping us understand how Abraham Lincoln felt about things that happened when he was alive. We had a lot of fun talking with him, and everyone agreed — Mr. Klein knows his subject!

45

After about an hour, we were ready to begin writing. We had to decide who our characters would be and where the story would take place. While we made suggestions, several "helpers"

were writing down our ideas. (Having more than one person taking notes helped to ensure that none of our great ideas were missed.) Mr. Lincoln sat in a nearby chair and answered questions as we worked. Whenever we got stuck or had too many good ideas, we voted.

We decided to have three kids on their way to the Abraham Lincoln Presidential Library to write a report for school. But outside the building, they ran into the real Abraham Lincoln! We had lots of ideas about how he could've gotten there, but we all agreed that in our story he would simply fall asleep and wake up in the future.

Sometimes we would get up and act out the story to help us get the dialog. Even Mr. Lincoln joined in, and we all had a great laugh when he jumped in the air like the president does in our story. Acting it out helped us decide what expressions our characters might have on their faces, and what they might say. Besides, acting it out was fun! We all got to take turns, and every author contributed.

It was pretty cool thinking about what the kids might do, and what President Lincoln would think about our world today. But when we talked about the way things might be if Abraham Lincoln had never been president, we realized what a difference he'd made. Mr. Lincoln was a very important man in our history, and we shouldn't take him for granted.

While we were writing, a professional illustrator began sketching out our characters. The illustrator for this book is Chuck Goll. He's from Chicago. The illustrator is the only adult who gets to make any suggestions, but Mr. Goll only interrupted to ask us questions. It was really cool to see the characters we'd described being drawn!

When we finished the story, we got a chance to draw our own illustrations and tell what we liked about writing this book. The whole experience was incredible! It was great learning more about Abraham Lincoln and cool meeting other young authors. We hope that you enjoy reading our story as much as we enjoyed writing it!

WeWrite Kids' Illustrations & Comments

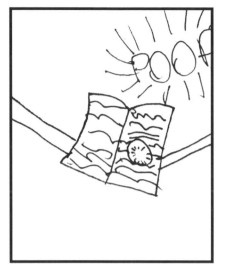

Erika Brodland
Age 7
(but turning 8 in 5 days)

"I liked acting it out and stuff like that. Well, I liked giving part of the story."

Sierra Brodland
Age 10

"I liked the part when they looked into the book and they could tell what's happening in the past. I like putting books together because I really like reading. I wish I could do it again."

Tyler Cameron
Age 9

"I liked the part of making up the story. I have made up stories at school. I want to be an author when I grow up."

WeWrite Kids' Illustrations & Comments

Emma Frederick
Age 9
(but going to be 10 in December)

"I learned a lot about Lincoln. Another thing I learned was getting to write a book that's actually going to be published. I've never written a book."

Kamaria Gage
Age 7 and a half

"The best part is when Lincoln has to go back to sleep to do his Gettysburg Address. It was fun to put blankets on him."

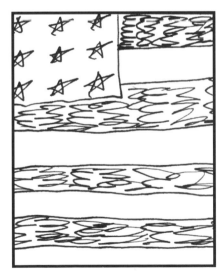

Isiah Hale
Age 10

"My favorite thing was acting the parts. I enjoyed writing this book."

WeWrite Kids' Illustrations & Comments

WeWrite Kids' Illustrations & Comments

Alyssa Henson
Age 7

"It was really funny. All these made-up names and stuff. It was fun to write the story and make up the story. The 'Yeah rights,' and 'I want to go home' were funny."

You may notice that Alyssa's drawing looks pretty professional. That's because it is! Since Alyssa is sight-impaired, illustrator Troy Freeman helped her out by drawing what she described. Thanks, Troy!

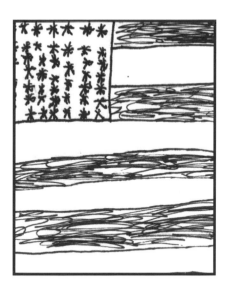

Lonnie Lucas
Age 9

"I had a good time working with other kids. I enjoyed writing this book."

Glen Morrison
Age 9

"It was a nice book. I recommend it to everybody out in the world if they want to know about President Lincoln."

WeWrite Kids' Illustrations & Comments

Joseph Stowell
Age 9

"I liked drawing. Yeah, I'm going to the library when it opens up."

Samuel Stowell
Age 10

"I liked acting stuff out."

Mily Vo
Age 9

"My favorite part was when Abraham Lincoln sat on the chair. He had a blanket on him and he faded away then everything went back."

WeWrite Kids' Illustrations & Comments

Linna Vo
Age 10

"I liked when Abraham Lincoln came to talk with us. I liked the end when he came back."

Matthew Wilde
Age 9

"I liked when Lincoln, I mean Fritz Klein, came because we got to ask him questions and he told us about Lincoln's life."

Illustrator at Work

Charles Goll has been an artist all his life. As a child, he used to trace cartoon characters from comic strips like Charles Schultz' Peanuts®, eventually learning how to draw them on his own. In high school, Chuck created his own comic strips based on the adventures of his group of friends. In college, he was the cartoonist for the student newspaper.

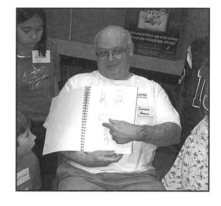

As a professional, Mr. Goll has done cartoons for numerous magazines. He's also worked with book publishers and greeting card companies. For a while he did technical illustrations for Encyclopedia Britannica.

Chuck Goll has been working freelance for over ten years, providing illustrations, cartoons, technical drawings, and animations for a wide variety of clients. *Mr. Lincoln and the Time Train* is Chuck's first project with WeWrite Corporation, but he's expected to do many more! **To see more of Chuck's work, visit his website at www.fallingsanta.com.**

The Story of Abraham Lincoln's Beard

It was the fall of 1860. Abraham Lincoln was the Republican nominee for President of the United States. Election Day was less than a month away. Mr. Lincoln, a lifelong beardless man, received a letter written by Grace Bedell, an 11 year old girl from Westfield, New York. Written October 15th, 1860, the letter urged him to grow a beard. Miss Bedell's unedited letter read:

NY
Westfield Chatauque Co
Oct 15, 1860

Hon A B Lincoln
Dear Sir

My father has just home from the fair and brought home your picture and Mr. Hamlin's. I am a little girl only eleven years old, but want you should be President of the United States very much so I hope you wont think me very bold to write to such a great man as you are. Have you any little girls about as large as I am if so give them my love and tell her to write to me if you cannot answer this letter. I have got 4 brother's and part of them will vote for you any way and if you will let your whiskers grow I will try and get the rest of them to vote for you you would look a great deal better for your face is so thin. All the ladies like whiskers and they would tease their husband's to vote for you and then you would be President. My father is going to vote for you and if I was a man I would vote for you to but I will try and get every one to vote for you that I can I think that rail fence around your picture makes it look very pretty   I have got a little baby sister she is nine weeks old and is just as cunning as can be. When you direct your letter dirct to Grace Bedell Westfield Chatauque County New York

I must not write any more   answer this letter right off
Good bye
Grace Bedell

The Republican Presidential nominee responded on October 19th.
His letter to Grace Bedell read:

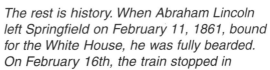

Private

Miss Grace Bedell
My dear little Miss.

Springfield, Ills.
Oct. 19, 1860

Your very agreeable letter of the 15th is received.

I regret the necessity of saying I have no daughters. I have three sons — one seventeen, one nine, and one seven, years of age. They, with their mother, constitute my whole family.

As to the whiskers, having never worn any, do you not think people would call it a piece of silly affection if I were to begin it now? Your very sincere well-wisher

A. Lincoln.

The rest is history. When Abraham Lincoln left Springfield on February 11, 1861, bound for the White House, he was fully bearded. On February 16th, the train stopped in Westfield, New York. The President-elect appeared on the train platform, and he called out for Grace. Grace was in the crowd with her two sisters, Alice and Helen. She came forth. Mr. Lincoln kissed her and told her he had taken her advice.

The Abraham Lincoln Center for Governmental Studies at the University of Illinois at Springfield commissioned WeWrite Corporation to create this book.

A Unique Process

WeWrite Corporation is a one-of-a-kind promotions agency, specializing in publishing **books written by kids for kids.** Using an exclusive workshop process, books are developed with children as co-authors.

Their story is professionally illustrated, edited, and put into book form. The WeWrite workshop approach is unique, offering children from all walks of life an amazing opportunity to become published authors.

WeWrite was founded in 1993 by Delores Palmer, a public library director. Her goal focused upon finding a way to hook kids into reading and writing. To date, the company has published more than 50 titles with a delightful discovery: Kids read more when they read WeWrite books, and often go on to write their own stories.

WeWrite Kids!™ books hold a special appeal: after all, who knows what will interest children better than the children themselves?

WeWrite Corporation believes that improving literacy levels of both children and adults is one of the best possible investments in the future of our growing global marketplace. WeWrite is committed to providing excellence in all of its publishing and marketing service areas.

To learn more about **WeWrite Corporation** and the books they've produced, visit their website at **www.wewrite.net,** or call **1-800-295-9037.**